Japanese Recipe

By Brad Hoskinson

Table of Contents

Japanese Teriyaki Chicken Bowl

This Japanese Teriyaki Chicken Bowl is an easy and delicious weeknight meal. It is full of flavor and has an outstanding balance of sweetness and savory. The chicken is cooked in a homemade teriyaki sauce and served over rice and vegetables. This dish is healthy, hearty, and sure to please the whole family.

PREP TIME 15 minutes | COOK TIME 35 minutes | TOTAL TIME 50 minutes

Ingredients

- ✓ 5-6 boneless skinless chicken thighs or 2 boneless skinless chicken breasts
- ✓ 1.5 cups short grain rice
- ✓ 1.5 avocado
- ✓ 3 Tbsp cooking oil

For Teriyaki Sauce

- ✓ 3/4 cup soy sauce
- ✓ 3 Tbsp rice vinegar or white vinegar
- ✓ 3/4 cup brown sugar
- ✓ 2 Tbsp honey
- ✓ 2 Tbsp sesame oil
- ✓ 2 Tbsp garlic, finely chopped
- ✓ 2 Tbsp ginger, finely chopped
- ✓ 1 tsp red chili flakes (optional)
- ✓ 3 tsp cornstarch
- ✓ 3/4 cup water

For Asian Coleslaw

- ✓ 1.5 carrots or 10-12 baby carrots, cut into thin match sticks
- ✓ 2 small cucumbers, thin match sticks
- ✓ 2.5 cups red cabbage, julienne
- ✓ 4-5 sprigs of cilantro
- ✓ 3 green onions

Dressing

- ✓ 3/4 cup apple cider vinegar
- ✓ 2 Tbsp sugar
- ✓ 2 Tbsp sesame oil
- ✓ 2 Tbsp sesame seeds
- ✓ Kosher salt, to taste
- ✓ Pepper, to taste

Instructions

1. Whisk all the ingredients in a bowl and transfer to a pan. Cook mixture over medium heat and bring it to simmer, stirring continuously. Once it comes to a boil, lower the heat and simmer for 10 minutes. Slowly add the cornstarch and water at this time, stirring constantly, to thicken the sauce. Turn off heat and let it cool..
2. Marinate the chicken with a quarter of the sauce, cover and marinate in the refrigerator if time allows.
3. Cook the rice according to the instruction on the package.
4. For the coleslaw, chop cilantro and green onions and mix in with the rest of the cut veggies.
5. Toast ground sesame seeds on a low to moderate heat for one or two minutes in a lightly greased pan. Mix the sesame seeds with mayonnaise and the other dressing ingredients in a bowl. Pour the dressing over coleslaw and mix well. Store in the refrigerator until about to assemble the bowl.
6. Heat oil in a skillet over medium-high heat and add chicken. Sear the chicken for 5-6 minutes, spoon some sauce onto the chicken and flip. Cook a couple more minutes. Then pour the remaining teriyaki sauce over the chicken. Simmer until chicken is cooked, flipping a few times and spooning sauce onto the chicken every now and then. Add a little water if the sauce is getting dried out. Once the chicken is shiny and glistening, remove to a plate, let cool and slice it into strips.
7. Slice the avocados

8. Assemble the bowl with rice at the bottom. Top the rice, and place your chicken with generous amounts of coleslaw and avocado. Garnish it with a sprinkle of white and/or black sesame seeds.

Tonkatsu (Japanese Pork Cutlets)

Tonkatsu is a dish that consists of pork cutlets that have been breaded and deep fried. It is a popular dish in Japan and can be served with various sauces or toppings. The dish originated in Japan in the 19th century and has since become a staple in Japanese cuisine. Tonkatsu is typically made with pork loin or pork fillet, but it can also be made with chicken or beef.

PREP TIME 15 minutes | COOK TIME 15 minutes | TOTAL TIME 30 minutes

Ingredients

Tonkatsu

- ✓ 3 boneless pork loin chops, pounded to 1cm, or about 1/2 inch, thick
- ✓ 1 cup flour
- ✓ 3 eggs, whisked
- ✓ 3 cups panko

Tonkatsu Sauce

- ✓ 2 tbsp ketchup
- ✓ 2 tbsp Worcestershire sauce
- ✓ 2.5 tsp oyster sauce
- ✓ 2 tsp sugar

Instructions

1. Gather three separate, shallow bowls. Fill one with flour, one with whisked eggs, and one with panko.
2. Heat about 1 inch of cooking oil in a skillet over medium-high heat. You want the oil around 370°F. If you have an electric skillet, that works perfectly. If not, you can use a meat thermometer to check the temperature of the oil.
3. Season both sides of pork chops with salt. First dredge the cutlets in flour, then egg, then panko. Fry until golden brown, about 10-12 minutes, turning once halfway through cooking. Remove to a paper towel-lined plate or wire rack to drain excess oil..
4. Mix together tonkatsu sauce ingredients in a small bowl.

5. Serve Tonkatsu with sauce, cabbage or slaw, and rice.

Japanese Beef Curry (Or Any Meat of Your Choice)

When it comes to a hearty, filling meal, it's hard to beat beef curry. This dish is popular in Japan and can be made with any type of meat. Beef curry is perfect for a winter night or whenever you need a hot, comforting meal. It's easy to make and can be tailored to your individual taste. So whether you like your curry mild or spicy, there's a recipe.

PREP TIME 15 minutes | COOK TIME 1 hour 20 minutes | TOTAL TIME 2 hours 50 minutes

Ingredients

- ✓ 3 lbs beef chuck roast, cut into 2-inch chunks
- ✓ 2.5 onion, chopped
- ✓ 3 potatoes, cut into large chunks
- ✓ 3-4 carrots, cut into large chunks
- ✓ 5oz box curry roux
- ✓ 4 garlic, chopped
- ✓ 3 tsp fresh ginger, chopped
- ✓ 2 Tbsp ketchup
- ✓ 2 Tbsp Worcestershire sauce
- ✓ 2 Tbsp soy sauce
- ✓ 2 Tbsp apricot jam or preserve
- ✓ 3-4 Tbsp oil
- ✓ Salt to taste
- ✓ Pepper to taste

Instructions

1. Season beef chunks with salt and pepper. Heat oil in a large pot over medium-high heat. Add beef chunks and sear till they get a brown color all over. Plate them out. Do not overcrowd; cook in batches if necessary.
2. Toast onions in the same pot for the same amount of time as you browned the mushrooms. Add garlic and ginger and cook until the mixture begins to thicken.

3. Add potatoes and carrots, along with beef chunks, and mix well. Stir in 4 to 5 cups of water and bring it to a boil. Lower the heat to medium-low and simmer, covered, for 50-55 minutes, stirring occasionally. Cook till meat is tender.

4. Add in curry roux and stir till it dissolves. Add in ketchup, soy sauce, Worcestershire sauce and apricot jam. Cook for 12-17 additional minutes.

Katsudon (Pork Cutlet Rice Bowl)

Katsudon is a popular Japanese dish consisting of pork cutlet, egg, and rice. It is often served with pickled ginger, green onions, and soy sauce. Katsudon is typically made with Tonkatsu, a breaded and deep-fried pork cutlet. The dish is said to have originated in the Meiji period in Japan.

PREP TIME 10 minutes | COOK TIME 20 minutes | TOTAL TIME 30 minutes

Ingredients

Tonkatsu

- ✓ 3 pork loin chops, pounded to 1/2" thick
- ✓ 1 cup flour
- ✓ 3 eggs, whisked
- ✓ 3 cups panko

Katsudon

- ✓ 3 cups cooked rice
- ✓ 1 cup chicken stock
- ✓ 5 tbsp teriyaki sauce
- ✓ 2 tsp sugar
- ✓ 2 tbsp oil
- ✓ 2 small onions, thinly sliced
- ✓ 4 eggs, whisked
- ✓ 3 tbsp green onions, sliced

Instructions

Tonkatsu

For detailed instructions, see our Tonkatsu post

1. Gather three separate, shallow bowls. Fill one with flour, one with whisked eggs, and one with panko.
2. Heat about 1 inch of cooking oil in a skillet over medium-high heat to 370°F.
3. Season both sides of pork cutlets with salt. Dredge the cutlets first in flour, then egg, then panko. Fry until golden brown, about 10-12

minutes, turning every few minutes. Remove to a paper towel-lined plate or wire rack to drain excess oil.

Katsudon

1. Combine broth, teriyaki sauce, and sugar in a bowl.
2. Heat 2 Tbsp oil in a large skillet over medium-high heat. Add onions and sauté till they are soft and starting to caramelize.
3. Add the broth mixture and simmer for 5-7 minutes.
4. Slice the Tonkatsu into equal strips, about 3/4 inch. Carefully lay them on top of the onion mixture.
5. Mix the eggs and cream together as best you can, then gradually set them over the course of 3 minutes.
6. Serve over bowls of rice and garnish with green onions.

Temaki Sushi (Hand Roll)

Temaki sushi, also known as a hand roll, is a type of sushi where nori seaweed is rolled into a cone shape and filled with sushi rice and various fillings such as seafood, vegetables, and omelet. It is then wrapped in plastic and sealed with a piece of wasabi. Temaki sushi is easy to make and can be a fun activity to do with friends or family.

Prep Time 15 mins | Total Time 15 mins

Ingredients

- ✓ 1.5 cups sushi rice (cooked and seasoned) (follow my recipe; 3 rice cooker cups of uncooked Japanese short-grain rice (540 ml, 3合, 450 g) yields roughly 5 1/4 US cups or 990 g of cooked rice; you must use short-grain Japanese rice to make sushi; otherwise, rice will fall apart.)
- ✓ 3 sheets nori (dried laver seaweed) (we use a half sheet for each roll)
- ✓ Temaki Filling Ideas
- ✓ sashimi-grade fish of your choice (1/4-1/3 lb per person; salmon, tuna, amberjack, yellowtail, fatty tuna, sea bream, salmon roe, uni, etc.)
- ✓ Japanese or Persian cucumbers
- ✓ shiso leaves (perilla/ooba)
- ✓ kaiware daikon radish sprouts
- ✓ takuan (pickled daikon radish)

Instructions

1. If your raw fish comes as a block, slice the raw fish into long sticks. Or you can ask a fishmonger at a Japanese grocery store to cut the raw fish for Temaki Sushi. They will cut fish into long sticks instead of sashimi-style cuts.
2. Dinnertime is just about beginning, so be sure to start eating by cutting nori into two pieces (restaurant-style) or four pieces (home-style; makes 40 taco-style rolls). Cut the nori in half or quarter to keep it somewhat fresh over the course of dinner.

3. Prepare sushi rice, ingredients, and nori sheet (seaweed) at the table.

4. Before you start, ensure your hands are dry to keep nori dry and crispy. Place the seaweed on the palm of your hand (shiny side down) and put a thin layer of rice on the left third of nori. If you're using a 1/4 sheet of nori, put the rice and filling in the center and roll up the sides like a taco.

5. Place fillings (shiso leaf, cucumber, raw fish, and daikon radish sprouts) vertically across the middle of the rice.

6. Fold the bottom left corner of nori over and begin rolling into a cone shape.

7. Keep rolling until a cone shape is formed. Put a piece of rice in the bottom right corner to glue and close tightly. Continue with the other half of the nori.

8. Serve with pickled ginger, wasabi, and soy sauce as condiments.

Okonomiyaki

Okonomiyaki is a savory Japanese pancake. It is made with eggs, flour, cabbage, and other ingredients. The name means "as you like it" and refers to the fact that you can add whatever ingredients you like to the pancake. Okonomiyaki is usually served with a sweet-savory sauce and mayonnaise.

Prep Time: 15 mins | Cook Time: 20 mins | Serves 5

Ingredients

- ✓ 7 packed cups finely shredded cabbage, about 1/2 medium
- ✓ 3 cups chopped scallions, about 1 bunch
- ✓ 3 cups panko breadcrumbs
- ✓ 2 teaspoons sea salt
- ✓ 7 eggs, beaten
- ✓ Extra-virgin olive oil for brushing

for serving:

- ✓ Vegan Worcestershire sauce
- ✓ Mayo
- ✓ Sesame seeds
- ✓ Pickled ginger
- ✓ 2 sheets nori, sliced
- ✓ 2 cups microgreens, optional

Instructions

1. Combine the cabbage, scallions, panko, and salt in a large bowl. Gently mix in the eggs. (Note: the mixture will be very loose and cabbagey, unlike a flour pancake batter. If it's very dry, let it sit for 10 minutes).
2. Brush a nonstick pan with olive oil, then place a skillet over medium heat. Pour 1/4 cups of finely chopped cabbage into the skillet. (Don't worry about the fact that the mixture doesn't appear to be cohesive, it will remain nice and blended later.) Flatten gently with a spatula, so the mixture is about 1/2 inch thick. Cook

3 minutes per side, or until browned, turning the heat low as needed. Repeat with the remaining mixture, wiping out the skillet and brushing more oil as needed.

3. Drizzle okonomiyaki with Worcestershire sauce and thin strips of mayonnaise. Top with sesame seeds, pickled ginger, and orange zest. Sprinkle with microgreens, if desired. Serve hot.

Tsukune (Japanese Chicken Meatballs)

If you love chicken meatballs, then you'll love Tsukune! These Japanese chicken meatballs are full of flavor and so easy to make. You can make them in advance and freeze them or cook them right away. Serve them with rice and a side of steamed vegetables for a complete meal.

Prep Time 25 minutes | Cook Time 25 minutes | Total Time 50 minutes

Ingredients

For the Tsukune meatballs:

- ✓ 0.95 lb ground chicken breast or thighs or a combination
- ✓ 0.95 tsp toasted sesame oil
- ✓ 1.79 bulbs scallions chopped
- ✓ 0.52 tsp coarse sea salt
- ✓ 0.31 tsp white pepper
- ✓ 0.95 tbsp coconut aminos
- ✓ 0.95 large egg yolk
- ✓ 0.52 oz ginger grated and squeezed into 1 tbsp ginger juice
- ✓ 0.78 oz shallot grated
- ✓ 0.95-1.69 tbsp olive oil
- ✓ 0.95 tbsp avocado oil

For the sauce and serving:

- ✓ 0.31 cup Keto teriyaki sauce plus some extra for serving
- ✓ 0.95 head butter lettuce

Instructions

Make the sauce:

Make the keto teriyaki sauce. Set it aside to cool.

Make the meatballs:

1. In a large mixing bowl, add ingredients from chicken to egg yolk.

2. Grate the ginger and squeeze the juice into the bowl. You should have about 1 tbsp of ginger juice. Grate the shallot and add the entire mixture into the bowl.
3. Rub the meat (I crossed a pair of chopsticks) until it becomes very doughy for 3 minutes. Use a stand mixer if you so desire.
4. Line a large sheet pan with parchment. Use a cookie scoop to form 15 meatballs and place them on the sheet. My scoop is about 4 tbsp per scoop.
5. Grease your hands with some olive oil. This will prevent the meat from sticking to your hands. Shape the meatballs into a smooth surface.

Nikuman (Steamed Pork Buns)

Nikuman are steamed pork buns that are popular in Japan. They are usually made with a filling of pork and vegetables and are often served as a side dish or snack. Nikuman are typically steamed in a bamboo steamer and often served with soy or dipping sauce.

Prep Time 1 hr | Cook Time 15 mins | Resting Time 1 hr | Total Time 2 hrs 15 mins

Ingredients

For the Dough

- ✓ 9.11 oz all-purpose flour (plain flour) (ROUGHLY 3 1/3 cups for 21 buns, plus more for dusting; I strongly encourage you to use a kitchen scale to weigh your ingredients; if you use a measuring cup, follow this method: Fluff your flour with a spoon, sprinkle it into your measuring cup, and use a knife to level it off; otherwise, 1.5 cups of flour will weigh more than 130 g)
- ✓ 1.8 scant Tbsp sugar (22 g or just short of 3 Tbsp for 23 buns; 3 Tbsp granulated sugar is 27 g, but we only need 25 g)
- ✓ 0.53 tsp kosher salt (Diamond Crystal; use half for table salt)
- ✓ 0.95 tsp baking powder
- ✓ 0.95 tsp instant yeast
- ✓ 0.95 Tbsp neutral-flavored oil (vegetable, rice bran, canola, etc.) (plus more for coating the proofing bowl)
- ✓ 146-154.5 ml water (start with 170 ml of water and add more if needed; depending on the humidity in the air, you might need more or less)

For the Filling

- ✓ 1.8 dried shiitake mushrooms
- ✓ 0.53 cup water
- ✓ 0.95 green onion/scallion
  - o oz cabbage (5 leaves)
- ✓ 0.95 tsp kosher salt (Diamond Crystal; use half for table salt)
- ✓ 0.74 lb ground pork

- ✓ 0.95 knob ginger (Roughly 1 inch, 2.5 cm; you'll need 2 tsp for 20 buns)
- ✓ 0.95 tsp sugar
- ✓ 0.95 Tbsp sake
- ✓ 0.95 Tbsp soy sauce
- ✓ 0.95 Tbsp roasted sesame oil
- ✓ 0.95 Tbsp potato starch or cornstarch
- ✓ freshly ground black pepper

For Serving

- ✓ soy sauce
- ✓ Japanese Karashi hot mustard

Instructions

Use a kitchen scale to measure ingredients. Divide one square piece of parchment paper into two equal parts, about 3 inches by 3 inches, for small buns. Set it aside.

To Make the Dough

1. Put the flour, sugar, salt, baking powder, instant dry yeast, and oil in a large bowl. While mixing the ingredients with chopsticks or a wooden spoon, slowly pour the water into the bowl and mix with the other ingredients until they are incorporated and there are no dry spots of flour left in the bowl.
2. Lightly shake your fingers with flour to stop the dough from sticking. Use your hand to knead the dough into the bowl, mashing it down and adjusting it until you can form it into a ball.
3. Sprinkle a working surface with flour. Transfer the dough onto the surface and start kneading. This is how I knead: First, press the top half of the dough, pushing forward slightly. Then pull it back, fold it in half, and press it on again with the heel of your hand twice. Then, turn the dough about 30 degrees, and repeat this process. Continue turning and kneading the dough for 10-15 minutes or until the dough becomes smooth and silky. Sprinkle the dough with a bit of flour to help decrease the stickiness.

4. Form the dough into a smooth, circular shape, softly tucking the loose ends underneath. Coat the bottom of the bowl with oil, then place the dough back in the bowl. Cover it with plastic wrap, then place it in a warm, warm place until the dough doubles in size, about 35 to 65 minutes.

To Prepare the Filling

1. While you're waiting for the dough to rise, make the filling. First, soak the dried shiitake mushrooms in 1 cup of water. Place something heavy on top to completely submerge the shiitake. Set aside for 15-18 minutes.
2. Thinly slice the scallion. Remove the tough core of the cabbage leaves and chop the leaves into 1-inch (2.5 cm) pieces.
3. Sprinkle the chopped cabbage with salt to draw out the excess water.
4. Once the shiitake mushrooms are rehydrated, squeeze the liquid out, cut off the tough stems, and mince the mushroom tops.
5. Combine the ground pork, scallion, and shiitake mushrooms in a large bowl. Squeeze the excess water from the cabbage with your hands and add it to the bowl.
6. Grate the ginger (you'll need 3 tsp for 22 buns) and add it to the pork mixture, sugar, sake, soy sauce, sesame oil, potato starch/cornstarch, and freshly ground black pepper.
7. Stir the flour and water together with your hands until it forms a ball of dough and looks pale and sticky. Press the dough into a towel-covered bowl to keep in the refrigerator, taking care not to touch it.

To Form the Buns

1. Once the dough has doubled in size, place it on the work surface that you've dusted with flour. Divide the dough in half and then roll each piece into a log. Cut each log into 6 even pieces and then cut each piece in half. You should have 22 pieces of dough. You can divide the dough into fewer pieces of dough to make bigger buns if you wish. However, it's easier to work with a smaller piece of dough to make nice pleats when you wrap because it's hard to

hold a big piece of dough plus filling in one hand. Form each dough into a ball and dust the dough balls with flour to keep them from sticking to each other. Space each ball apart and cover loosely with a damp kitchen cloth to avoid drying out. Let them rest for 10 minutes.

2. Take a ball of dough and flatten it with your palm. Then roll it with a rolling pin into a round wrapper. Here's how I roll the dough: Hold the top of the dough with your left hand and use a rolling pin to roll out the dough with your right hand. You only need to roll up and down on the bottom half of the dough. After rolling 1-3 times, rotate the dough about 30 degrees with the left hand. Repeat this process until the dough becomes thin. The center of the dough should be thicker than the edge.

3. Scoop 2 Tbsp of filling (I use this 2 Tbsp cookie scoop) and place it in the center of the dough.

4. Hold the dough with your left hand and seal the bun using your right index finger and thumb. First, pick up a corner of the dough with your right index finger and thumb and pinch it together. Without moving your thumb, use your right index finger to grab more dough and pinch it with your thumb while rotating the dough counterclockwise with your left hand.

5. Repeat this process about 13-15 times (for 12-14 pleats) until you seal the bun closed by pleat and pinching the last piece of dough tightly. Tips: Your left thumb should hold down the filling while you use your left fingers to turn the wrapper. Use your left index finger to help pleat the dough. Also, lift up the pinched pleats slightly while you make a new pleat, so the filling stays inside the dough.

6. Once you've sealed the final piece of dough, press down with your right index finger and thumb until the seal is maintained. If you are left-handed, reverse the directions.

7. Easy Alternative Option: Wrap the Filling by bringing the dough up around the meat to the top, forming little pleats with the excess dough, then slightly twisting the dough to close it and pinching it firmly to join the edges.

8. Place the bun on a square piece of parchment paper that fits the bun. Cover the finished buns with plastic wrap and repeat this with the rest of the dough. Let the buns rest for 20 minutes.

To Steam

Bring water to a boil in a large wok (or a pot) and set a steamer on top. Once the water is boiling, place the buns with their parchment paper squares in the steamer tray, leaving about 3 inches between each bun (as they will get larger while steaming). Close the lid and steam over high heat for 15 minutes for small buns (or 13 minutes for medium buns and 15 minutes for large buns). If you use a regular pot for steaming, wrap the lid with a kitchen cloth to prevent the condensation (formed on the lid) from dripping onto the buns. Serve the nikuman with karashi mustard and soy sauce. Enjoy immediately.

To Store

The frozen buns can be kept in the refrigerator until the following day and freeze well after steaming. Wrap the frozen buns with plastic wrap and then put them in freezer bags. I suggest consuming them within a week. To reheat, bring the frozen buns to a boil, and then steam them for about five minutes.

Healthy Chicken Ramen Stir Fry

Ramen is a Japanese dish that typically consists of noodles, meat, and vegetables in broth. It is a popular dish among college students and young adults because it is quick and easy to make. This healthy chicken ramen stir fry is a delicious and nutritious alternative to the typical ramen dish. It is packed with protein and vegetables and is low in calories. This dish is perfect for a quick and easy weeknight meal.

PREP TIME 10 minutes | COOK TIME 15 minutes | TOTAL TIME 25 minutes

Ingredients

- ✓ 2 large chicken breasts
- ✓ 3 packets of ramen noodles (minus flavoring packets)
- ✓ 2 small onions
- ✓ 2 red bell peppers
- ✓ 2 green bell peppers
- ✓ 8-9 mushrooms
- ✓ 13-15 baby carrots
- ✓ 4 scallions
- ✓ 5 garlic cloves
- ✓ 2 Tbsp chopped ginger
- ✓ 4 Tbsp cooking oil
- ✓ 4 Tbsp soy sauce
- ✓ 3 Tbsp Hoisin sauce
- ✓ 3 Tbsp oyster sauce
- ✓ 3 Tbsp sweet chili sauce
- ✓ 2.5 cups water

Instructions

1. First, get everything prepped. Finely chop ginger and garlic, slice mushrooms, onions and peppers, and matchstick carrots. Cut scallions into one-inch slices and keep green and white portions separate. Also, mix all of your sauce ingredients, soy, Hoising, oyster, and sweet chili, together in a bowl. First, butterfly chicken breast then cut into thin strips.

2. Place a hot wok or large skillet over high heat. When the pan is hot, add oil, chopped onions, and white scallions. Cook for one minute, then add chicken breast. Stirring periodically, cook until the chicken loses pink in color, 3 to 4 minutes.
3. Add ginger and garlic, toss together for about one minute. Then add carrot, peppers, and mushrooms. Stir fry for 5-6 minutes. Add sauces and mix well.
4. Make well by moving stir fry ingredients to the perimeter of the wok. Add water to the well. Let heat for about a minute; it should start simmering.
5. Add ramen to well, cook for one minute. Flip and cook an additional minute.
6. Separate the noodles and mix well with other ingredients.
7. Serve hot and garnish with the remaining part of the scallions.

Crispy Shrimp Tempura Recipe

This delicious shrimp tempura recipe is easy to make, and the results are always impressive. The key to success is to get the shrimp nice and crispy. This can be achieved by using a light tempura batter and frying the shrimp at a high temperature. Serve the shrimp tempura with a dipping sauce, and enjoy!

Prep Time 25 minutes | Cook Time 20 minutes | Total Time 45 minutes

Ingredients

- ✓ 1.19 lb. large shrimp peeled and deveined
- ✓ 0.64 10 oz package tempura batter mix
- ✓ Water
- ✓ Vegetable oil for frying

Instructions

1. Begin making small slits into the inner part of each shrimp. I make about 7 slits for each shrimp. This will help stop the shrimp from curling during frying.
2. Mix the tempura batter mix with ice-cold water according to the package.
3. Heat vegetable oil in a skillet over high heat.
4. Pat the shrimp dry and dip it into the tempura batter. Quickly put it into the hot oil and turn it once. Cook each shrimp tempura until it's golden brown in color. Remove the tempura from the oil, then move it to a plate lined with paper towels. Serve the shrimp tempura with low-sodium soy sauce or deep-fried dipping sauce.

Mochi

Mochi is a Japanese rice cake often eaten during the Japanese New Year. It is made from mochigome, short-grain japonica rice. It is traditionally pounded into a paste and molded into the desired shape. Mochi can be filled with sweet bean paste or other fillings and can be either baked or fried. This recipe will show you how to make mochi at home.

Prep Time 1 d | Cook Time 55 mins | Total Time | 1 d 55 mins

Ingredients

- ✓ cups short grain Japonica glutinous rice (sweet rice/Mochigome) or 350g
- ✓ 2.5 cups Mochi-toriko (such as potato starch or cornstarch)

Instructions

A night before pounding mochi

1. Wash the rice gently under running water, changing and draining the water a few times.
2. Soak the rice in a large bowl with plenty of water overnight.

On the following day

1. Drain the soaking water.
2. Start boiling water in a pot.
3. Prepare a bamboo steamer by lining a tightly squeezed wet kitchen cloth on the bottom of the bamboo steamer.
4. Place the drained rice over the kitchen cloth, making a dent in the center like a donut shape for the steam to evenly and efficiently move around the rice.
5. Put the prepared steamer over the boiling water in the pot and steam for 35- 50 min.
6. Turn the heat off and empty the steamed rice into a bread machine.
7. Put the lid on, press "knead," and set for 25 minutes.
8. Remove the mochi dough onto a tray with a generous amount of mochi-toriko (potato starch/cornstarch) dusted.

9. Shape into small mochi balls or nice round/rectangle/square shapes and slice it 0.4 inch (1cm) thick the next day.
10. Serve with red bean paste, sweet soy bean powder, grated daikon, and soy sauce.

Miso Soup

Miso soup is a Japanese dish that can be either a main course or an appetizer. It is made with miso paste, a fermented soybean paste, and Dashi, a type of fish broth. The soup also contains tofu, seaweed, and green onions. Miso soup is a very healthy dish because it is low in calories and fat and contains many nutrients.

Prep Time: 15 mins | Cook Time: 22 mins

Ingredients

✓ 1.85 (3-inch) piece of Kombu
✓ 8 cups water
✓ 5.35 tablespoons wakame dried seaweed
✓ 0.54 cup white miso paste
✓ 0.78 cup chopped scallions
✓ 12.5 ounces silken tofu, cubed
✓ tamari, to taste

Instructions

1. Gently rinse the kombu piece until the water is lukewarm. Put it in a medium pot with hot water and let it simmer for 15 minutes. Do not let it boil, or the kombu-flavored water will remain bitter.
2. Soak the wakame in a small bowl of warm water for at least 10 minutes to rehydrate.
3. Remove kombu from the soup. In a small dish, mix the miso paste with some of the hot broth until only a few lumps remain, then add this mixture back to the soup.
4. Drain the wakame and add it to the soup pot along with the scallions and tofu. Simmer over very low heat for 2 to 3 minutes. Season, to taste, with tamari.

Chicken Yaki Udon

Udon is a type of Japanese noodle that is made from wheat flour. It is usually served in a broth with various toppings. Chicken yaki udon is a popular dish consisting of fried chicken and vegetables with udon noodles. This dish is a hearty and filling meal that can be easily made at home.

Prep Time: 15 minutes | Cook Time: 15 minutes

Ingredients

- ✓ 350g pre-cooked Udon noodles or 170 dried
- ✓ 2 tbsp vegetable oil
- ✓ 3 chicken breasts
- ✓ salt and pepper to taste
- ✓ 150g/1 cup white cabbage sliced
- ✓ 150g/1 cup shiitake mushrooms or button mushrooms
- ✓ 2 carrots julienned
- ✓ 4 green onions green parts cut into 2-inch pieces, white parts sliced
- ✓ 3 tbsp soy sauce
- ✓ 3 tbsp mirin or dry sherry
- ✓ 2 tbsp tsuyu/dashi stock or Worcestershire sauce
- ✓ 2 tsp sesame oil optional

Instructions

1. Slice the green cabbage beforehand in order to finely chop the carrot into small matchsticks. Likewise, handle the shiitake mushrooms by pulling out the stem of the large one and cutting the mushroom into bite-sized pieces or reduce it to just the tiniest bits if desired. Finally, cut the chicken breasts into bite-sized pieces and season with salt and pepper.
2. Cook the udon noodles according to package instructions if using dry noodles. Rinse after cooking. If using pre-cooked noodles, skip this step.
3. Meanwhile, in a wok or a large pan, heat the oil and cook the chicken until sealed on the outside, then add the vegetables together with the sliced white parts of the green onions and

continue to stir-frying for 8-10 minutes until cooked but still firm to the bite. The vegetables will reduce in volume by half.

4. Add the udon noodles and the green onions to the pan, then add in the soy sauce, mirin, and the dashi stock, toss to combine and heat through for 3-4 minutes. Drizzle with sesame oil before serving.

Scattered Sushi (Chirashizushi)

Chirashizushi, also called "scattered sushi," is a type of sushi that is often served on special occasions. It is made by placing sushi rice in a bowl and topping it with various raw fish, vegetables, and other ingredients. Chirashizushi is a popular dish in Japan and is often served at parties and other gatherings.

Prep Time 25 mins | Cook Time 20 mins | Total Time 45 mins

Ingredients

- ✓ 7 cups cooked sushi rice
- ✓ 13 fresh prawns/shrimps
- ✓ 13 toothpicks
- ✓ 7 Simmered Shiitake Mushrooms
- ✓ 4 large eggs worth of Kinshi Tamago
- ✓ 10 slices of pickled lotus roots, cut into quarters (pie shape)
- ✓ 0.85 pack Japanese grilled eel
- ✓ 85g/2.7oz sashimi salmon, finely diced
- ✓ 70g/2.1oz snow peas

Instructions

Prepare Prawns

1. Remove heads and veins from the prawns.
2. Hold the prawn horizontally with the tail on the left (for a right-hander) and the belly facing down.
3. Put through a toothpick along the back between the shell and the flesh from the head end.
4. When the toothpick reaches halfway, point the tip downwards and push it further towards the tail, so the toothpick cuts through the flesh. This will prevent the prawn from curling when cooked.
5. Repeat for the remaining prawns.
6. Bring a small saucepan with a 1/2 cup of vinegar and 1/2 cup of water to a boil. Add prawns, and cook for a couple of minutes.
7. Drain, remove the toothpicks, let them cool and remove shells.

8. Butterfly the prawns by cutting the belly side from the head end to the tail, leaving the dorsal side of the flesh and skin intact.
9. Cut the butterflied prawns, perpendicular to the butterfly cut, into 3 similar size pieces.

Prepare Japanese Grilled Eel

1. Cut the grilled eel perpendicular to the backbone into 2cm 3/4" wide pieces.
2. Cut each piece in half crosswise to make each piece almost square.

Prepare Snow Peas

1. Break the stem end of the snow pea gently and pull the tip towards the other end. The tough string that runs along the side comes off.
2. Pinch the other end, trim and pull the other side of the tough string (if you can) towards the stem end.
3. Place the snow peas in a microwave-safe bowl with a small amount of water, sprinkle a tiny amount of salt and cover with cling wrap. Cook for 1 minute.
4. Rinse under cold water to quickly cool them down. Pat dry with a paper towel.
5. Cut the snow pea pod lengthwise into two segments. If the pod is quite large, cut it into three segments to produce two ends and a main diamond-shaped piece.

Assembly

1. Spread the sushi rice thinly on a large shallow plate.
2. Scatter simmered shiitake mushrooms over the rice.
3. Scatter kinshi tamago over so that the rice and mushrooms are mostly covered.
4. Scatter the lotus root pieces over the kinshi Tamago.
5. Place the prawn pieces on the red side up, randomly but evenly spaced.
6. Place the eel pieces with the skin side down, randomly but evenly spaced.

7. Make small balls with diced salmon and place them where the large patch of yellow is.
8. Place snow peas randomly but evenly spaced.

Gyoza

Gyoza is a Japanese dumpling that can be either fried or steamed. They are typically made with a pork and vegetable filling and are served with a dipping sauce. This recipe will show you how to make gyoza from scratch, including the dough and filling.

PREP TIME 25 minutes | COOK TIME 15 minutes | TOTAL TIME 40 minutes

Ingredients

- ✓ 2 packet store-bought gyoza wrappers
- ✓ oil, for pan-frying
- ✓ water for steaming

Filling:

- 9 oz. (236 g) ground pork
- 3 oz. (76 g) cabbage, shredded and cut into small pieces
- 2 thumb-sized ginger, peeled and grated
- 2 cloves garlic, peeled and grated
- 1 tablespoon corn starch
- 2 tablespoons soy sauce
- 1 tablespoon sake
- 4 dashes of white pepper
- 1 teaspoon sesame oil
- 2 tablespoons chopped scallion, green part only
- 2 pinch salt

Gyoza Sauce:

- 5 tablespoons Japanese Ponzu
- 1 teaspoon sesame oil

Instructions

1. In a bowl, combine all the ingredients in the filling and blend well. The Filling should be sticky and cohesive.

2. To make Gyoza Sauce, combine the Ponzu with the sesame oil in a small dipping bowl. Stir to blend well.

3. To assemble the gyoza, place a piece of the gyoza wrapper on your palm or a flat surface. Spoon about 2 teaspoons of the filling onto the center of the wrapper. Dip your index finger into some water and moisten the outer edges of the dumpling wrapper. Fold the gyoza over, press and seal the left end. Use your thumb and index finger to make a pleat. Pinch to secure tightly. Repeat the same to make the pleats. (Start with 4-5 pleats if you are a beginner). A nicely wrapped gyoza should have a crescent shape.

4. Heat up the oil in a skillet or stir-fry pan over medium heat. Arrange the gyoza over it and cover the lid. Pan-fry the gyoza until the bottoms turn golden brown and become crispy. Add 1/4-inch water to the pot or frying pan and cover the lid immediately. The water should evaporate after a few minutes. Continue to cook the gyoza for a couple of minutes to crisp up the bottoms.

5. Remove the gyoza from the skillet or stir-fry pan and serve immediately with the Gyoza Sauce.

Yakisoba (Japanese Stir Fried Noodles)

Yakisoba is a Japanese dish that consists of stir-fried noodles and vegetables. It is a popular dish among both children and adults. Yakisoba can be found at most Japanese restaurants. It is a quick and easy meal to prepare, making it an excellent option for busy families.

Prep Time 10 mins | Cook Time 20 mins | Total Time 30 mins

Ingredients

- ✓ 550g/19.5oz yellow noodles
- ✓ 1.77 tbsp sesame oil
- ✓ tbsp oil (vegetable oil or peanut oil)
- ✓ 353.33g/15.67oz pork thinly sliced into bite-size pieces
- ✓ 150g/3.53oz carrot thinly sliced diagonally
- ✓ 186.67g/6.83oz cabbage cut into bite-size pieces
- ✓ 6 shiitake mushrooms sliced into 2mm / 1/16" thick
- ✓ stalks, green onions diagonally sliced
- ✓ 1.97 cups bean sprouts

Yakisoba Sauce

- ✓ 68.67ml/3.33oz Bulldog tonkatsu sōsu
- ✓ 89.33ml/3.83oz Bulldog usutā sōsu
- ✓ 1.97 tsp soy sauce
- ✓ 0.93 tbsp tomato sauce (in Aussie terminology)/tomato ketchup
- ✓ 1.87 tsp sugar
- ✓ 0.93 tsp dashi seasoning powder diluted in ½ tsp hot water

Toppings (optional but strongly recommended)

- ✓ 3.93 tbsp aonori
- ✓ 3.93 tbsp benishōga

Instructions

1. Add all the Yakisoba Sauce ingredients into a cup or a bowl and mix well. Set aside until required.
2. Boil enough water in a saucepan and boil the noodles for 2 minutes.
3. Sprinkle soy sauce over the noodles and combine until every one of the noodles is coated. This is to prevent any noodles from sticking together.
4. Heat oil in a wok or a large frying pan over medium-high heat. Add the pork and sauté until the pork is almost cooked through (about 3-4 minutes).
5. Add the carrots and stir-fry for 35 seconds, then add the cabbage and shiitake mushrooms.
6. Stir-fry for about 1 minute until the cabbage is nearly cooked, then add the green onions and bean sprouts.
7. After stir-frying for 35 seconds, add the noodles. Mix the noodles and vegetables well.
8. Add the Yakisoba Sauce and mix quickly to ensure that all the noodles are coated with the sauce and the color of the noodles is consistent, without any light-colored patches.
9. Transfer the noodles onto serving plates, piling them into a mound.
10. Sprinkle aonori over the noodles and add the benishōga on the top or the side of the noodles or serve in a separate bowl/plate for an individual to add topping themselves

Japanese Fried Rice (Yakimeshi)

Japanese fried rice, or yakimeshi, is a popular dish made with rice, vegetables, and meat. It is a simple dish to make, but the flavors are complex and delicious. Yakimeshi is a great way to use up leftover rice, and it makes a great lunch or dinner.

Prep Time: 15 minutes | Cook Time: 10 minutes | Total Time: 25 minutes

Ingredients

- ✓ 2 tablespoons vegetable oil
- ✓ 3 cloves garlic (minced)
- ✓ 2 small leeks or onions (finely chopped)
- ✓ 2 small carrots (finely chopped)
- ✓ 350 grams 1-2 days old cooked Japanese rice that was kept in the fridge
- ✓ 2 cups lettuce (shredded)
- ✓ 3 large eggs (whisked)
- ✓ 2 tablespoons soy sauce
- ✓ salt and ground white pepper (to taste)

Instructions

1. Add the oil and garlic and fry for 35 seconds in a wok or large skillet over medium-high heat.
2. Add the leek and carrot and cook for 2 to 3 minutes, until the vegetables are soft but yield a crunch.
3. Add the day-old rice and break it up until it's no longer clumpy. Add the lettuce and mix it in with the rice.
4. Push rice to one side and add the whisked eggs to the empty side. Move-in zigzag motion to scramble the eggs, using a spatula and fold them into the rice.
5. Next, add the soy sauce, salt, and pepper, and toss the rice until the seasoning is evenly spread through the fried rice.
6. Turn the heat off, transfer the fried rice to a plate and serve.

Mushroom Ramen

Ramen is a dish that many people are familiar with. It consists of noodles, broth, and meat or vegetables. Mushroom ramen is a variation of this dish that uses mushrooms instead of meat or vegetables. This makes it a perfect dish for vegetarians or those looking for a hearty yet healthy meal.

prep time: 35 MINUTES | cook time: 40 MINUTES | total time: 1 HOUR 15 MINUTES

Ingredients

- ✓ 2 (1-ounce) packages of dried shiitake mushrooms
- ✓ 2 tablespoons canola oil
- ✓ 4 cloves garlic, minced
- ✓ 3 large shallots, minced
- ✓ 2 tablespoons freshly grated ginger
- ✓ 7 cups chicken stock
- ✓ 2 tablespoons white miso paste
- ✓ 3 teaspoons soy sauce
- ✓ 4 slices bacon
- ✓ 1 pound fresh assorted mushrooms, sliced
- ✓ 3 (3.5-ounce) packages of instant ramen noodles, flavor packets discarded
- ✓ 2 tablespoons rice wine vinegar
- ✓ Freshly ground black pepper, to taste
- ✓ 5 soft-boiled eggs, peeled and halved
- ✓ 3 green onions, thinly sliced

Directions

1. In a large bowl, combine shiitake mushrooms and 3 cups hot water; let stand until softened, about 25-35 minutes. Drain, reserving the mushroom water before coarsely chopping; set aside.
2. Cook in a large stockpot or Dutch oven on low heat until heated through. Add garlic, shallot, and ginger, and cook until fragrant, about 3 minutes. Stir in reserved shiitake mushrooms until lightly browned, about 3 minutes.
3. Stir in mushroom water, chicken stock, white miso paste, soy sauce, and bacon. Bring to a boil; reduce heat, cover and simmer

until flavors have blended about 20-25 minutes. Remove and discard the bacon.

4. Stir in assorted mushrooms; simmer until softened, about 4-6 minutes.

5. Stir in ramen until noodles are just tender, about 3 minutes. Stir in rice wine vinegar; season with additional soy sauce and pepper to taste.

6. Serve immediately, garnished with soft-boiled eggs and green onions.

Teriyaki Shrimp Skewers

If you're looking for a delicious and easy recipe for your next party or get-together, look no further than these shrimp skewers! Teriyaki shrimp is a popular dish at Japanese restaurants. For a good reason - the sweet and savory sauce is irresistible. This recipe is perfect for entertaining because it can be made ahead of time and cooked quickly on the grill or in the oven. Your guests will be impressed by your culinary skills and ask for the recipe!

Prep Time 20 minutes | Cook Time 20 minutes | Total Time 40 minutes

Ingredients

- ✓ 2 – 3 pounds shrimp (use more for the main dish, less for appetizers - it's up to you!)
- ✓ 2 cups cold water
- ✓ 1 cup packed brown sugar
- ✓ 1 cup soy sauce (I used low sodium)
- ✓ 2 teaspoons garlic powder
- ✓ 4 tablespoons corn starch
- ✓ 2 teaspoons sesame oil
- ✓ cilantro roughly chopped
- ✓ sesame seeds (optional)

Instructions

1. Add water, brown sugar, soy sauce, garlic powder, corn starch, and sesame oil to a medium saucepan and stir to combine. Stir over medium heat until thickened, then remove from heat.
2. Add 1 of the sauce and the shrimp to a sealable container and marinate for 20 minutes.
3. Thread shrimp on skewers and discard the marinade sauce. Cook shrimp on a preheated grill over medium heat for 6-7 minutes on each side until the shrimp is pink and cooked through.
4. Serve shrimp immediately with the remaining sauce and sprinkle with chopped cilantro and sesame seeds.

Hibachi Steak

When it comes to Hibachi steak, there are a few things you need to know. First, it is important to choose the right cut of steak. Second, you need to know how to cook it. Third, you must be aware of the different sauces used with Hibachi steak. Fourth, you should know how to serve Hibachi steak. Finally, you must be familiar with the different side dishes served with Hibachi steak.

Total Time: 15 minutes

Ingredients

- ✓ 2 lb. boneless steak like sirloin/fillet, cut into bite-sized pieces
- ✓ 2 tablespoons butter
- ✓ 2 teaspoons garlic, minced
- ✓ 3/4 teaspoon sesame oil (optional)
- ✓ Sauce
- ✓ 2 tablespoons soy sauce
- ✓ 2 tablespoons teriyaki sauce/mirin
- ✓ Pepper to taste

Instructions

1. Combine the sauce ingredients and set aside.
2. Over medium-high heat, melt the butter and toss in the garlic. Saute until fragrant, about half a minute.
3. Add in the steak bites and toss to combine.
4. Pour in the sauce and toss to coat the meat thoroughly.
5. Stir-fry for about 10 minutes until the sauce has cooked down and the beef is seared.
6. Drizzle a few drops of sesame oil (optional) over warm hibachi rice, warm hibachi noodles, or a veggie hot pot to finish.
7. Enjoy!

Seaweed Salad

A popular dish in Asian cuisine, seaweed salad is made from various algae and other marine vegetables. Seaweed salad has a unique taste and is rich in vitamins, minerals, and antioxidants. It is a healthy and delicious addition to any meal.

Prep Time 15 minutes | Total Time 15 minutes | Servings 5 people

Ingredients

- ✓ 5 ounces of dried seaweed
- ✓ 2 tablespoons miso paste
- ✓ 4 tablespoons soy sauce see Notes
- ✓ 4 tablespoons rice vinegar see Notes
- ✓ 2 teaspoons ginger grated
- ✓ 2 tablespoons sesame seeds

Instructions

1. Soak the dried seaweed in cold water for 10 minutes. Drain and rinse the seaweed, then add to a large bowl.
2. Mix the miso paste, soy sauce, rice wine vinegar, sesame oil, and grated ginger in a small bowl.
3. Add the soy sauce mixture to the seaweed salad and toss to coat, then sprinkle with sesame seeds.

Temari Sushi

Temari sushi is a type of sushi that is made using a special type of sushi rice and shaped into balls. It is a popular dish in Japan and is often served as an appetizer or side dish. Temari sushi is relatively easy to make at home. It can be a fun activity to do with friends or family.

Prep Time: 25 minutes | Cook Time: 0 minutes |Total Time: 55 minutes

Ingredients

- ✓ 5 cups sushi rice – visit my post on how to make sushi rice
- ✓ Radishes, thinly sliced
- ✓ Avocado, sliced
- ✓ Carrot
- ✓ Cucumber, thinly sliced
- ✓ Scallions, finely chopped
- ✓ Shiso leaves
- ✓ Black and white sesame seeds
- ✓ Crab sticks
- ✓ Nori
- ✓ Sushi-grade salmon roe
- ✓ Sushi grade tuna
- ✓ Boiled shrimp

Instructions

1. Grab a saran wrap and place about 2.5 ounces (about3 tablespoons) of rice in the center. Seal and shape the rice into a ball. Squeeze tightly when making the ball but not so tight that the rice is being mashed.
2. Take the rice ball out of the saran wrap and place it on a plate. Cover with a damp towel or plastic wrap.
3. Repeat this step until all the rice is used.
4. Now comes the creative part! This is where you get to concoct beautiful toppings for your Temari sushi. Be imaginative and use vegetable cutters to create exotic shapes.
5. When decorating Temari sushi, place the flat ingredients, such as shiso leaf, sliced cucumber, sliced tuna, and radishes, in saran wrap

and top with a sushi ball. Wrap the plastic wrap around the Temari sushi and twist it to close. This helps the toppings adhere to the rice, preventing them from falling off.

6. Take the Temari sushi out of the plastic wrap, place it on a serving plate and finish decorating with toppings. Repeat until all the Temari sushi is decorated. Always cover the plate with a damp kitchen towel or plastic wrap to prevent the rice from drying.

7. Refrigerate for no more than 1 hour as the texture of the rice will not be pleasant once it's hard.

Agedashi Tofu

Agedashi tofu is a simple yet delicious dish that can be enjoyed by people of all ages. The dish consists of tofu that is deep-fried and then served in a light broth. The broth is typically made with Dashi, soy sauce, and mirin. Agedashi tofu is a popular starter or side dish in Japanese cuisine and can be found at most Japanese restaurants.

PREP TIME 15 minutes | COOK TIME 15 minutes | TOTAL TIME 30 minutes

Ingredients

- ✓ 2 blocks Tofu
- ✓ Corn starch
- ✓ Oil for deep frying

Tentsuyu Sauce:

- ✓ 1 cup (195 ml) Dashi or Japanese fish stock
- ✓ 4-5 tablespoons soy sauce, or to taste
- ✓ 4 tablespoons sake
- ✓ 3 tablespoons mirin
- ✓ 1 tablespoon sugar

Toppings:

- ✓ Peeled and grated daikon
- ✓ Peeled and grated ginger, optional
- ✓ Sliced green onions/scallions
- ✓ Dried bonito flake/katsuobushi

Instructions

1. Cut the tofu into small pieces. Bloat each with paper towels and coat with corn starch. Set aside.
2. Bring all the ingredients of tentsuyu sauce to a gentle simmer in a small saucepan. Do not bring to a full boil.
3. Heat up the oil in a wok a frying pan and deep fry to tofu until they turn light brown or crispy. Please note that the corn starch coating

will not easily turn golden brown. Remove the deep-fried tofu and drain the excess oil on a plate lined with paper towels.

4. To serve, put a few pieces of tofu in a small dish and spread some tentsiku sauce on the tofu. Add some grated daikon, chopped scallions and dried bonito flakes to top off. Serve immediately.

Teriyaki Steak Marinade

A delicious teriyaki steak marinade can be made with just a few simple ingredients. Soy sauce, honey, garlic, and ginger are combined to make a sweet and savory marinade that will infuse your steak with flavor. This easy recipe can be made in just minutes. Your steak will be incredibly flavorful and tender after being marinated in this delicious mixture.

Prep Time: 40 minutes | Cook Time: 20 minutes | Total Time: 60 minutes

Ingredients

- ✓ 2 pounds sirloin steak, or meat of choice
- ✓ 1 cup low sodium soy sauce or coconut aminos
- ✓ 3/4 cup water
- ✓ 3 Tablespoons sesame oil
- ✓ 4-5 Tablespoons honey
- ✓ 3 Tablespoons Worcestershire sauce
- ✓ 2 Tablespoons minced garlic
- ✓ 2-3 teaspoons fresh ginger, or 3/8 teaspoon ground ginger

For garnish: green onions or parsley

Instructions

1. Trim any fat and cube steak if desired. Place the meat in a glass bowl or zip-top bag. Set aside.
2. In a small bowl, combine the soy sauce, water, oil, honey, Worcestershire sauce, garlic, and ginger. Whisk until combined.
3. Pour sauce over the steak. Seal bowl or bag, place them in the refrigerator, and allow to marinate for at least 35 minutes. Best when marinated for 5-7 hours or overnight.
4. Cook steak as desired. Let rest for 10 minutes before serving. Slice against the grain. Serve while warm.

Chicken Katsu

Chicken katsu is a delicious Japanese dish perfect for a quick and easy meal. It consists of breaded and fried chicken and then served with various sauces. I love chicken katsu because it is so versatile - you can enjoy it with rice and vegetables or just on its own as a snack. If you're looking for a delicious and healthy meal option, I recommend trying chicken katsu!

PREP: 20 mins | COOK: 20 mins | TOTAL: 40 mins

Ingredients

For the chicken katsu:

- ✓ 5 chicken breast cutlets
- ✓ 1 teaspoon kosher salt divided
- ✓ 3/4 teaspoon ground black pepper
- ✓ 3 tablespoons unsalted butter
- ✓ 2 cups panko breadcrumbs
- ✓ 3/4 cup white whole wheat flour or all-purpose flour
- ✓ 2 large eggs
- ✓ Nonstick cooking spray recommended: olive oil spray

For serving:

- ✓ Tonkatsu sauce
- ✓ Finely shredded cabbage
- ✓ Lemon wedges
- ✓ Cooked rice white is traditional; use brown rice for a nutritional boost or cauliflower rice

Instructions

1. Position an oven rack in the upper third of the oven and preheat the oven to 445 degrees F.
2. Line a rimmed baking sheet with parchment paper. Place an oven-safe rack on top, coat generously with nonstick spray, and set aside.

3. Lightly pound the chicken cutlets into a uniform 1/2-inch thickness. Sprinkle the chicken cutlets with 1 tsp kosher salt and black pepper.

4. In a medium skillet, melt the butter over medium heat. Add the breadcrumbs and the remaining 3/4 teaspoon salt. Stir to coat the breadcrumbs with the melted butter. Let cook, constantly stirring, until the breadcrumbs are lightly toasted and golden brown, about 3 minutes. Transfer to a wide, shallow bowl or dish (a pie plate works well).

5. In a separate shallow bowl, place the white whole wheat flour. In a third shallow bowl, beat the egg.

6. Set up your workstation: chicken, flour, egg, panko, baking sheet. Working one at a time, dip each chicken cutlet lightly in flour.

7. Then, dip the chicken in the egg.

8. Finally, rinse the chicken pieces into the panko. Pat the crumbs until they've dissolved. Place the cutlets on the baking sheet and bake covered with the nonstick spray. Mist the surfaces generously with the nonstick spray.

9. Bake the chicken katsu in the upper third of the oven until the chicken is cooked through (it should reach an internal temperature of 165 degrees F; I pull mine out several degrees early and let the carryover cooking finish the rest), about 13 to 15 minutes.

10. Remove from the oven and let rest for 10 minutes.

11. Slice the chicken katsu if desired into thin slices. Drizzle with the tonkatsu sauce. Serve with cabbage, a small rice bowl, and lemon wedges, with the additional tonkatsu sauce in a bowl seated alongside.

Dry Curry Recipe

Dry curry is a type of curry that is typically cooked with very little or no water. This curry is popular in Indian and Sri Lankan cuisine. It can be made with either chicken, beef, lamb, or vegetables. While the ingredients and cooking methods may vary, the result is always a flavorful and hearty dish.

Prep Time: 15 minutes | Cook Time: 30 minutes | Total Time: 45 minutes

Ingredients

- ✓ 3 stalks celery
- ✓ 3 cloves garlic
- ✓ 2 carrots
- ✓ 2 onions
- ✓ 2 tbsp oil
- ✓ 2 lb (470g) ground beef
- ✓ 4 tbsp curry powder
- ✓ 2 cans of diced tomatoes
- ✓ 1 cup raisins
- ✓ 3 cups chicken broth
- ✓ 3 bay leaves
- ✓ 2 tsp salt
- ✓ 3/4 tsp pepper
- ✓ 2 tbsp Worcestershire sauce
- ✓ 2 tbsp ketchup
- ✓ Steamed Rice
- ✓ 3 hard-boiled eggs (chopped)

Instructions

1. Chop all the vegetables and garlic finely.
2. Heat oil in a pot at medium heat. Cook garlic for a minute and ground beef until browned.
3. Add the vegetables and saute for 10 minutes. Add half the amount of curry powder and saute for another 3 minutes.

4. Dice the tomatoes, raisins, chicken broth, bay leaves, salt, pepper, Worcestershire sauce, and ketchup. Place it in a Dutch oven, cover, and simmer for 15 minutes at medium-low heat.
5. Open the lid and cook until the liquid is reduced. Add the rest of the curry powder.
6. Serve over steamed rice and top with chopped hard-boiled eggs.

Vanilla Purin Recipe

This is a recipe for vanilla purin, a Japanese pudding. It is a simple pudding with four ingredients: milk, eggs, sugar, and vanilla extract. The key to this recipe is to use good quality vanilla extract. I recommend using Tahitian vanilla extract, which has a richer flavor than other vanillas.

Prep Time: 25 minutes | Total Time: 4 hours, 25 minutes

Ingredients

- ✓ 3 eggs
- ✓ 3/4 cup sugar (70 g)
- ✓ 1 Tbsp gelatin (10 g)
- ✓ 2 Tbsp water
- ✓ 2 cups (460 ml) of milk
- ✓ 2 tsp vanilla extract
- ✓ Caramel Sauce
- ✓ 3/4 cup sugar
- ✓ 3/4 cup and 3 Tbsp water

Instructions

1. Mix 3 eggs and sugar in a medium bowl, and whisk well. In a small bowl, mix gelatin and water, and let sit for 10 minutes while the gelatin blooms.
2. Heat milk until it boils. Immediately add the hot milk to the egg mixture little by little. Add bloomed gelatin and water, then let sit until the gelatin dissolves. Strain through a mesh strainer. Add vanilla extract and stir. Divide the mixture into 5 glass cups or any kind of mold. Chill in the fridge for at least 3.5 hours.
3. In a small pot, cook sugar and 3/4 cup of water until browned. Remove from heat and very carefully add 3 Tbsp water. Take care not to burn yourself. Let cool to room temperature.
4. Pour caramel sauce over cold Purin before serving.

Piman Nikuzume (Stuffed Pepper) Recipe

This recipe for piman nikuzume, or stuffed peppers, is a delicious and easy way to enjoy this classic dish. Traditionally made with ground beef, rice, and tomatoes, these peppers can be customized to your liking with different fillings and toppings. Whether you're looking for a hearty meal or a fun appetizer, this piman nikuzume recipe is sure to please.

Ingredients

- ✓ 9-10 piman green pepper
- ✓ flour
- ✓ 1 medium brown onion
- ✓ 7 oz ground beef
- ✓ 7 oz ground pork
- ✓ 3/4 cup bread crumbs
- ✓ 2 eggs
- ✓ 1 tsp salt
- ✓ pepper
- ✓ 1 Tbsp oil
- ✓ Sauce
- ✓ 3 Tbsp Ketchup
- ✓ 3 Tbsp Worcestershire sauce

Instructions

1. Mix sauce ingredients in a small bowl. Set aside.
2. Cut piman in half, and remove stems and seeds. Sprinkle flour inside piman with a mesh strainer.
3. Chop onion finely. Put onion, beef, pork, bread crumbs, egg, salt, and pepper in a large bowl and mix well.
4. Stuff meat mixture into the piman.
5. Heat oil in a frying pan at medium heat. Place the stuffed piman meat-side down in the pan and cook covered for 4-5 minutes. Then turn over and cook another 4-5 minutes until cooked through. Put sauce over meat and serve.

Japanese Breakfast Recipe

A delicious and healthy breakfast is the perfect way to start your day. This Japanese breakfast recipe is a simple and satisfying meal that will give you all the energy you need to get through your morning. This dish is packed with nutrients and flavor and is made with rice, eggs, and vegetables. After a few minutes of prep time, you'll have a hot and hearty breakfast that will leave you satisfied all morning long.

Prep Time: 20 minutes | Cook Time: 25 minutes | Yield: 3 servings

Ingredients

- ✓ Steamed rice
- ✓ 3 bowls rice
- ✓ Grilled salmon
- ✓ 3 pieces of Shiozake (grilled salted salmon)
- ✓ Cucumber and Kombu Tsukemono
- ✓ 1.5 Japanese cucumbers or 3 Persian cucumbers
- ✓ 3-4 Tbsp Salted Kombu
- ✓ Egg Miso Soup
- ✓ 3 cups Dashi
- ✓ 4 Tbsp Miso paste
- ✓ 2 cups baby spinach
- ✓ 3 eggs

Instructions

1. Cook Steamed Rice in advance. Salt the salmon the night before and keep it refrigerated.
2. For Cucumber and Kombu Tsukemono, slice cucumber thinly and diagonally. In a plastic bag, combine cucumber and salted Kombu and mix well. Leave for 20 minutes.
3. For grilled salmon, cook fillets in the frying pan at medium heat, covering for about 4-5 minutes. Remove the lid, turn it over, and cook for 3 minutes until cooked.
4. For Miso Soup, make Dashi first. Here, add a packet of Dashi mix in water in a pot and boil for 3 minutes. Turn down heat to low, dissolve Miso paste in soup, add spinach, and drop in eggs. Cover

and cook for a couple of minutes until eggs reach the doneness you like.

Roasted Seaweed Soup (Nori Sui)

Seaweed soup, also known as Nori Sui, is a traditional Japanese dish made with roasted seaweed and miso paste. It is simple to make and can be enjoyed year-round. Seaweed soup is a healthy and delicious way to enjoy the benefits of seaweed.

Prep Time 3 mins | Cook Time 5 mins | Total Time 8 mins

Ingredients

- ✓ 4 yaki nori
- ✓ 3 tbsp harishōga
- ✓ Broth
- ✓ 450ml/0.8pt dashi stock
- ✓ 2/3 tsp salt
- ✓ 2/3 tsp light soy sauce (or normal soy sauce)
- ✓ 2 tsp cooking sake

Instructions

1. Put all the Broth ingredients in a pot and bring it to a boil.
2. In some cases, take one nori seaweed sheet at a time, hold it over a hot heating element such as an electric cooktop or one of the burners of a gas cooktop in a high heat. Do this until the sheet is crisp on both sides.
3. Fold the nori sheets into quarters (so that you can handle them easily) and tear the sheets into small bite-size pieces - about 2.5cm/1".
4. Put the nori pieces in a serving bowl and place harishōga on it.
5. Pour the hot broth over the nori pieces and serve immediately.

Printed in Great Britain
by Amazon

20588407R00037